STUPID THINGS
MEN DO

STUPID THINGS MEN DO

Man and Mind
in Perfect Harmony

Compiled by

ANDREW JOHN

Michael O'Mara Humour

First published in Great Britain in 2000 by
Michael O'Mara Books Limited
9 Lion Yard, Tremadoc Road
London SW4 7NQ

www.mombooks.com

A CIP catalogue record for this book is available
from the British Library

ISBN 1-85479-564-3

3 5 7 9 10 8 6 4 2

Designed and typeset by Martin Bristow

Printed and bound in Great Britain
by Cox & Wyman Ltd, Reading, Berks

CONTENTS

INTRODUCTION

For some reason, when we think of sheer stupidity we think of men. Women are seldom in the history books or books of records or all the little books of nonsense you find in the bookshops. They tend on the whole to be more sensible.

Perhaps it's to do with the male's questing, hunting instincts: he's always ready to go off and try something different – even if it means being utterly stupid. The female – more sensibly 'right-brained' and intuitive – rarely feels the need to get up to these silly and often dangerous tricks.

So we've brought together in this little book some of the most absurd, stupid, foolish, idiotic, insane, crazy, mad, lunatic, senseless, fatuous, ridiculous, ludicrous, asinine, witless deeds from some of the most simple-minded, dim-witted, deranged, unhinged, demented, cracked, cuckoo, dotty, dippy, downright bonkers men on Planet Earth.

Don't read it while walking on the top of a cliff or crossing a busy road, there's a good chap.

ANIMALS

Animals – many of them man's best friend – can be a source of humour and often the nemesis of stupid men. Like the gerbil that reached the parts other gerbils just don't reach, or the elephant that needed to offload . . .

Death squad

There was a firemen's strike in 1978 and the British Army had to fill the firemen's boots, as it were. One day they were called to the home of an elderly woman in South London, whose cat had become trapped in a tree. Where else?

The woman was so grateful that the soldiers had arrived in such haste that she asked them if they'd like to come in for some tea. There being no other emergencies to attend to, they gladly accepted her invitation. Having taken their fill of tea and dainties, the cat-loving soldiers drove off waving to the old woman as she stood on her doorstep – and ran right over the rescued cat. Splat!

Fangs ain't what they used to be

The Victorian traveller Charles Waterton was fascinated by the vampire bat, and had spent many years studying the creature. But he felt that scientific rigour demanded he be bitten by one. So he slept with one in his bedroom and allowed his big toe to be exposed.

However, many weeks passed and the big toe remained untouched by the tiny fangs. But his Indian servant, Richard, had been nightly ravaged by the bat and became too weak to work.

'His toe held all the attractions,' Waterton once said.

Ribbet, ribbet . . .

A Glasgow man thought some ornamental frogs for his garden pond would be just the thing – but he decided he wanted a touch of realism, and bought some hi-tech ones that were equipped with voices. They were movement-sensitive and let out a very convincing croak. Unfortunately, they kept it up all night and neighbours complained.

Eventually, Andrew Cromar was brought before Glasgow District Court accused of causing annoyance, and was fined £150. The three frogs were present throughout the hearing.

Snake's alive!

A man called Gordon, who comes from Darwin in Australia, allowed a snake to bite him nine times in 1999. He had to be revived three times on an operating table after an encounter with a king brown, thought to be the 21st most deadly venomous snake in the world.

Gordon has admitted to having been drunk at the time. He was driving to Darwin with a friend when they saw the snake, and Gordon decided to pick it up. The snake immediately bit his hand, but he withstood the pain long enough to place the snake into a plastic bag, which he tossed into the back of his car.

Gordon, for some reason he admits was stupid, decided to stick his hand back in the bag. 'It must have smelled blood, and it bit me another eight times,' he said.

He was taken by ambulance to hospital, and his friend tried to keep him conscious by 'whacking me in the head and pouring beer on me'.

As a result of the poison, Gordon lost an arm and the use of his legs, and the hospital said it would be a long time before he regained full muscle control.

Just when you thought it was safe to go back in the water . . .

A chap was fishing on Marathon Beach, Florida, with friends in July 1999 when he saw fins in the sea, and immediately thought, Dolphins! And he jumped in.

Then he discovered that the fins belonged not to dolphins but to sharks. His friends fished him out somehow, and he was treated in hospital for shark bites.

Trunk load

Friedrich Riesfeldt, a zookeeper in Paderborn, Germany, felt the pressing need in 1998 to feed his constipated elephant more than the recommended dose of animal laxative. He gave Stefan 22 doses plus a bushel of berries, figs and prunes.

And the laxatives did their work only too efficiently. Without being too graphic about it, let's say that the accumulated waste matter from the bunged-up animal was expelled with a great deal of force, and the keeper, aged 46, was suffocated under 200 pounds of poo.

A Paderborn policeman, Erick Dern, told reporters, 'The sheer force of the elephant's unexpected defecation knocked Mr Riesfeldt to the ground, where he struck his head on a rock and lay unconscious as the elephant continued to evacuate his bowels on top of him.

'With no one there to help him, he lay under all that dung for at least an hour before a watchman came along, and during that time he suffocated. It seems to be just one of those freak accidents that happen.'

Up, up and away

This tale concerns two guys in Salt Lake City whose sexual exploits with a toilet-roll tube and a gerbil left little to the imagination.

The story came from a website devoted to stupid things men do, and all the stories are claimed to be true. This one *seems* a little unlikely, but you never know. I'm sure stranger things have happened.

Eric Tomaszewski told doctors at Salt Lake City Hospital Burns Unit in 1998: 'In retrospect, lighting the match was my big mistake. But I was only trying to save the gerbil.'

Tomaszewski and his partner Andrew 'Kiki' Farnum had been indulging in a practice called 'felching', which, in this instance, involved Tomaszewski's putting a cardboard toilet-paper tube up Farnum's rectum and slipping the gerbil, Ragout, in.

'As usual, Kiki shouted out "Armageddon", my cue that he'd reached Nirvana, so to speak. I tried to retrieve Ragout but he simply would not come out, so I peered into the tube and struck a match, thinking the light might attract him.'

Tomaszewski's story came out at a hushed press conference, when a hospital spokesman described what happened next. 'The match ignited a pocket of intestinal methane gas in Kiki's colon. Flames shot out the tube, igniting Mr Tomaszewski's hair and severely burning his face. They also set fire to the gerbil's fur and whiskers, causing it to scurry further up Kiki's colon, which in turn ignited a larger pocket of gas further up the intestine, propelling the rodent out of the cardboard tube like a cannonball.'

He explained that Tomaszewski had suffered second-degree burns and a broken nose from the impact of the gerbil, while Farnum suffered first- and second-degree burns to his anus and lower intestinal tract. The gerbil didn't survive.

Please don't try this one at home.

CORPORATE STUPIDITY

Men don't have to be on their own to be utterly stupid. They can do it in groups. In fact, they often do it better than way. Great minds and all that.

Now, before irate men start writing to the publisher saying there were women on the team, too, yes, we know! But most of you, most of the time, are men. And therefore your team, group, board of directors or whatever is fair game.

Accidents will happen

In 1968 the Royal Society for the Prevention of Accidents (ROSPA) held an exhibition.

The entire display collapsed.

Creating the 'missing link'

Our preoccupation with genetically modified crops and biological manipulation during the late 1990s and early 2000s is nothing compared with what the Chinese were up to in 1980. They tried to impregnate female chimps with human sperm, so they could develop a hybrid for menial chores.

Dr Qi Yongxiang of the city of Shenyang said the hybrids could also provide substitutes for human transplant organs. And the Chinese authorities said there need be no qualms about killing such a creature, since it would be classed as an animal.

Well, that's one bit of monkey business we haven't heard any more about.

Dishing the dirt

Scientists at Newcastle in the north-east of England just could not work out why their pollution readings were so high. After all, Newcastle may be a city – subject, like any other urban environment, to its fair share of dust and fumes – but surely not the most polluted city in the country, possibly even the world?

Then it dawned on the batty boffins that their state-of-the-art, hugely expensive monitoring equipment was sited right over a lorry park!

Flight of fancy

The guys who dreamed up Canada's federal flight regulations must have had a severe case of jet lag. It is an offence, for instance, to enter a plane while it is in flight. And you cannot leave an aeroplane while it is in flight – unless you wish to make a parachute jump. Anyone found jumping from an aeroplane without a parachute will be committing an offence.

Going at it head on

The Pakistani Islamic sect of Tebrik-a-Nifaz decided in May 1994 that devout Muslims should drive on the right-hand side of the road. Followers, as you would expect, did just as their leaders ordered.

But everyone else in Pakistan drives on the left, and this, as you might imagine, caused one or two problems. So a fortnight later the sect issued another decree rescinding the previous one, because there had been so many accidents.

Gunning for trouble

The Mitrailleuse machine-gun was the first of its kind – sophisticated, deadly, a truly state-of-the-art piece of hardware. And, what was more, it was one of the best-kept secrets of the Franco-Prussian War (1870–1).

Indeed, the secrecy surrounding this astounding item of equipment was such that no instructions were issued on how it worked until the first day of the war. By then, of course, the chaps on the front line were thinking about other things!

Hooked on law and crime . . .

Ohio newshounds must have uncovered a real can of worms when they tackled this story. The state's Wildlife Division spent more than $25,000 in pay trying to find a notorious criminal. Three weeks of surveillance was carried out by fourteen agents and two undercover agents. They took photos from secret hiding places and bought products undercover from the crook.

But the 'criminal' turned out to be an eight-year-old boy who had been selling bait illegally. He had a stand outside his parents' house and sold worms to passing fishermen. He'd obviously sold some to the occasional undercover agent, too.

The case was dismissed – although Ohio taxpayers were faced with a bill equivalent to the cost of 27 tons of worms.

Good going, guys. Now go and pick on someone your own size.

Non compos mentis

When the state of Florida passed its 'English-only' law, officials within its counties were not allowed to offer services in a foreign language.

In their wisdom, officials of Dade County decided that the zoo should stop including Latin names of animal species on its signs.

Solving that particular problem must have been something of a *pons asinorum* for those chaps, what?

It figures . . .

Dallas City Hall had on display three small figurines as part of an exhibit. However, they were nude, and officials thought this might offend some people. So they had the figurines' vital bits covered with little hand-made fig leaves.

Now *there's* an appreciation of art!

Keeping abreast of the times

Houston City Council in Texas decided in 1990 that they would draft an ordinance to outlaw shows of bare women's breasts in public.

But they wanted to make sure the language of the new rule was just right, so they hired a researcher whose sole task was to discover and detail why women's breasts were different from men's.

Well you see, fellas, there were these birds and these bees . . .

Nutty as a fruitcake

In 1994 the state government of Pennsylvania brought in a bill to outlaw the 'libelling' of fruit, vegetables and seafood. Under this measure, manufacturers and sellers, as well as growers, of perishable food could 'attempt to recover damages for the disparagement of any such food product or commodity'.

You rotten tomato, you! You slippery banana skin!

It's always most embarrassing when you live in a glass house but are caught throwing stones. Britain's Health and Safety Executive was established in 1974 for the express purpose of dealing with safety. Its remit included checking safety standards in the workplace.

But in 1987 staff at its London office went on strike over . . . you've guessed it: safety. The HQ was deemed unsafe, causing one union spokesman, Don Street, to declare, 'This place is a deathtrap.'

The Notting Hill headquarters underwent renovation, but Mr Street's members had daily to dodge flying glass and falling masonry – as well as colliding with careless workmen carrying planks round corners. Oh, and there were plenty of power cables to trip over.

The climax of it all was when a piece of scaffolding came crashing through a glass roof and on to a clerk's desk.

Plane potty!

It was hardly surprising that the chaps at the National Aeronautics and Space Administration (NASA) couldn't find anyone to help them with their latest idea for an experiment.

They wanted to make a scientific study of what it would be like to have the noise of a jet aeroplane blasted into private homes for fourteen hours a day.

Perhaps they should just live under the flight path at Heathrow!

Not quite to the letter

You'd think the Post Office would get it right. But they were feeling pretty stupid in 1986 when they launched a quiz competition with just one question: What is your postcode?

As a promotion to get people to remember their postcodes, it was a good idea. However, when giving their address, the Post Office got their own postcode wrong.

They said it was a printing error. Shall we give them the benefit of the doubt? No! Why the hell should we?

Sporting chance of survival

Long Island Lighting Company in New York wanted to be seen to be doing the right thing, knowing how sensitive people are about nuclear power. They told the Nuclear Regulatory Commission that their evacuation plan in the event of an accident at their Shoreham power plant would be for residents to be evacuated immediately to the Nassau Coliseum.

Unless there was a ball game or other attraction on at the time, of course.

You gotta get your priorities right, guys, after all.

The heat got to him

State Representative John Galbraith of Ohio decided to reduce the use of energy by introducing a bill to abolish January and February. 'If we divide the fifty-nine extra days between July and August, we will cut our energy needs by about one-third through eliminating the coldest days of the year,' he said. 'Cold is largely a psychological matter. If people look at the calendar and see that it is July, they will be quite happy to turn the heat down.'

Nice idea, John. Try it in Alaska.

Top of the cops for dumbness

It's said that the Philadelphia Police Department was the inspiration for the Keystone Kops. No one could touch them for sheer stupidity, it seems. In 1830 a special law had to be passed to stop them from falling asleep on duty.

Uniforms had to be introduced in 1840 after a group of rioters refused to recognize Patrolman Bramble as a police officer, so scruffily was he attired. The entire force didn't like the idea of uniforms, and refused to wear them for ten years – not encouraged even by the Mayor of Philadelphia, who wore a helmet to public meetings as an inducement to the men to do likewise.

Because none of the officers would work on Sundays, this was the day when crime rose to its weekly peak.

History hasn't taught them, it seems: in 1987 a report showed that they exhausted themselves unnecessarily by dashing from one unimportant call to another with sirens screaming.

And when they launched 'Operation Grandpop' – during which officers dressed as derelicts in order to attract muggers – they arrested hundreds of innocent people, including an elderly shoeshine boy.

Scouting for thrills

A Scout leader in Florida must have been in search of a unique adventure in July 1999 when he went missing from home for 36 hours.

The 42-year-old was reported missing by his wife, and more than 40 deputies searched for him on foot, on horseback and from helicopters.

Eventually, he was found hanging upside down and stark naked but for his shoes, with a video camera positioned to capture his exploits.

Investigators could only speculate on what happened. It seems he had wanted to film an auto-erotic situation, but, having got the footage he required, he was too tired to pull himself back up in order to free himself from the ropes. So he had to hang upside down until rescuers found him.

His injuries were so severe that his left foot had to be amputated.

Sergeant Nick Pallitto of the Lane County Sheriff's Department commented, 'Some things are better confined to your own home.'

When the wind blows . . .

A newspaper in the north of England advised its readers that, in the event of a four-minute warning of nuclear attack, they should paint their windows with a mixture of whitewash and curdled whey to deflect the deadly rays. Oh, and they should soak their furniture with a mixture of borax and starch.

And all in four minutes.

Travellers' tales

OK, so some of this sorry tale comes down to bad luck, but there's enough stupidity here to make it worth the telling – and you can bet most of the organizers were men.

It was the occasion of the 1985 annual conference of the Association of British Travel Agents (ABTA), held in Sorrento. First, the conference train was delayed by a points failure at Purley, the flight was late, there was fog at Gatwick and most people arrived a day late.

Then people began to go down with food poisoning – so many, in fact, that the ABTA doctor was given special praise in the closing address. His skills were called upon when two people fell down a marble staircase and the marketing director of Kuoni Travel was bitten by a snake.

Then came the annual golf tournament – but everyone arrived to find that organizers hadn't realized that there wasn't a golf course in Sorrento.

So this event had to be postponed and held in Dublin.

The climax of the conference was to be when the Italian Minister of Development addressed all the delegates in the forum at Pompeii, when a local travel agent called Lucio Aponte was to fly over the site and drop 3,500 roses on the visitors.

Nice thought. But the light aircraft swooped unexpectedly on the delegates, drowning out the minister's words. The roses were dropped, but missed the forum completely.

The plane reappeared and dropped some more. They missed – but it had swooped so low that the delegates felt the need to crouch. And a third attempt was equally unsuccessful, as were the fourth and fifth. However, Mount Vesuvius looked distinctly pretty covered in roses!

TOO CLEVER
BY HALF

Doesn't it make you feel good to know that even the clever sods can cock it up sometimes? Don't you get that wonderful feeling of *schadenfreude* when some smart arse gets his comeuppance? Take the arty types who thought they were ever so appreciative of good art and possessed the last word in taste, until they learned who – or what – the artist was. Or the boffins who discovered that we eat because we are hungry.

Statue or bust!

The novelist A. N. Wilson probably felt just a little stupid after he caused a right old hornets' nest by complaining bitterly that there was no memorial bust of Matthew Arnold (1822–88), the British poet and literary critic, in Poets' Corner in Westminster Abbey.

He fired off letters pointing this out, and even organised a petition, headed by the biographer

Victoria Glendinning and Auberon Waugh, editor of the *Literary Review*.

Ever the crusading journalist, Waugh wrote that 'Arnold's reputation has stood the test of time, and continued exclusion seems shameful'. And he suggested his readers join the campaign and write letters to the Dean of Westminster.

When the Dean received his barrage of letters, he courteously – probably unable to suppress a smile as he did so – replied to each writer, pointing out that there was a very lifelike bust of Matthew Arnold, thank you very much, and it had been in the Abbey since 1891.

Good in parts

The unknown author who sent his manuscript for appraisal to Dr Samuel Johnson (1709–84), the English poet, critic, essayist and lexicographer, must have felt pretty stupid when he got the learned man's reply.

It read, 'Your manuscript is both good and original. But the part that is good is not original, and the part that is original is not good.'

Country pursuits

Ed Zern of *Field and Stream* magazine was asked by his editor to choose a book to review. Believing that *Lady Chatterley's Lover* – which had been tried for obscenity – contained much to interest the country type, that was the title he went for.

The book does indeed contain details of country life and work, but it contains a lot else too, not least of which are the rather explicit sexploits of the game-keeper and his boss's wife. *Lady Chatterley's Lover*, he wrote, had just been reissued by Grove Press and

> this fictional account of the day-by-day life of an English gamekeeper is still of considerable interest to outdoor-minded readers, as it contains many passages on pheasant-raising, the apprehending of poachers, ways to control vermin, and other chores and duties of the professional gamekeeper. Unfortunately, one is obliged to wade through many pages of extraneous material in order to discover and savour these side-lights on the management of a Midland shooting estate, and in this reviewer's opinion this book cannot take the place of J. R. Miller's *Practical Gamekeeping*.

Stupidity as an art form

Even those who claim refined artistic judgement can be downright stupid – and the chances are that most of them are men. A display of the works of a new and exciting artist called Yamasaki was held in Frankfurt in 1978, and the artist was lauded as 'the discovery of the year'.

Organizers spoke of the 'luminosity of his colours' and the 'excitement of his powerfully dynamic brushwork'. All 22 exhibits were quickly snapped up for £500 each.

Then it was announced that the artist would make a guest appearance – and the art 'lovers' realized their stupidity when a chimp was brought in.

Behrend Feddersen, one of the organizers, said, 'I encouraged him to throw paint on twenty-two canvases.' Whereupon he announced that the money would be donated to the circus where Yamasaki worked.

Perhaps, though, these discerning cultural types would be consoled to know that during the last quarter of 1961 *Le Bateau*, a painting by Henri Matisse (1869–1954), hung upside down in a gallery at the New York Museum of Modern Art, and 116,000 people saw it and didn't notice. The painting depicted a sailing boat, and the reflections of the summer clouds could be seen in the water. Hence the mistake.

The error was eventually noticed by the artist's son.

What a fascinating bucket!

The publications officer at the Victoria and Albert Museum in London thought it would be a good idea to have 5,000 postcards printed. Would probably help the funds.

The picture he chose riveting, scintillating, fascinating: a fourteenth-century Tibetan rain bucket.

As far as we know, only a handful were ever sold.

Journo jerks

Ross and Kathryn Petras in their funny paperback *The One Hundred Stupidest Things Ever Done* (Michael O'Mara, 1997) recount the story of the stupid student journalists at Arizona State University in 1995. They were given a quiz, say the writers, 'including names that every aspiring journalist should recognize'. Here are some of the answers:

Alzheimer's: Imported beer
Apartheid: A building in Athens
Louis Armstrong: The first man on the moon
Count Basie: A vampire
Jesse Jackson: The leader of the Moral Majority

Yawn value

In *The Book of Heroic Failures* (Routledge and Kegan Paul, 1979), Stephen Pile, its author, tells the story of a pretty stupid competition that only men could devise. It was held annually at Leeds University to find the most stultifyingly boring talk. The university's Dr David Coward won the 'Boring Lecturer of the Year' contest two years running. This is how Pile tells the tale:

Lecturers nominate themselves and may speak on any subject. Dr Coward, a lecturer in the French Department, set the record in 1977 with a delightfully dull talk on 'The problem of the manned urinal'. In winning, he fended off such slight opposition as a man who feel asleep during his third sentence amidst boos and catcalls, and a member of the medical faculty whose lecture 'How to tell right from left' was repeatedly illustrated by slides of a billiard ball viewed from different angles.

The previous year Dr Coward had won with a Marxist explanation of a joke about coconuts. 'It wasn't a terribly good joke,' he said, 'but after I had explained it for twenty minutes people began to see its latent merits.' He retired from the competition undefeated.

Hungry for facts

A study by the fellows at Taiwan's Council for Agricultural Planning and Development revealed the startling fact that people eat lunch because they are hungry.

They also found out that some people ate lunch because they ate three meals a day – and lunch was one of them.

It's amazing what you can find out if you really try.

Faux pas

Language has been known to get many people into hot water – not least among whom was Sir Richard Posnett, the English president of the town-twinning arrangement between Godalming in Surrey and Joigny in France.

Posnett got things off to a shaky start at the twinning ceremony in 1985 when he greeted the French visitors with a speech in which he used the verb *baiser*. Now all he meant was that he'd 'kiss all your women'. But *baiser* has taken on a different meaning since Posnett was at school, and is now somewhat taboo. Today it often means to fornicate with, and the French party were horrified to think he was going shag all their women.

Lice work if you can get it

This one could also have qualified for our section on sport, but I decided it should go with other dotty professors and the like. Dr Terence Glanville, whose specialist study at the University of Nottingham was wood lice, decided that racing the creatures would be a good idea.

So he devised a ten-lane track for them, and the idea was that they would have numbers painted on their backs.

If the course was covered with a damp cloth, this would increase the speed of the lice.

All this was in 1984, and Glanville saw a great future for his new idea.

ON THE ROAD – AND OCCASIONALLY OFF IT

Men can be at their most stupid when behind the wheel of a vehicle. Like the man who failed his driving test before it began, or the guy who was just dying – literally – to retrieve his car keys.

Not all the anecdotes here concern cars: some concern other forms of travel.

Going for a spin

A 63-year-old man and his 64-year-old woman companion were driving along Newell Highway near Moree in north-western New South Wales in 1997 when their car collided with something.

What it crashed into was the side of a fully laden train about 600 metres long. Which even a 63-year-old man with chronic myopia should have seen.

It was not a happy story, for the train moved off

although the car had become wedged between two carriages. It was dragged and travelled more than a kilometre and a half before it approached an unfenced bridge with a ten-metre drop. Just before the car reached the precipice, it struck a pylon, dislodging it from the train. It spun several times before coming to rest. Lucky escape.

However, with only minor bruising to show for his ordeal the Queensland motorist set off on foot for help, but managed to slip on the bridge, falling to his death below.

Driving ambition thwarted by a toot

Most of us failed to pass our driving test on the first attempt. But to fail before the examiner even gets into the car? Yet it happened.

In 1981 a Lanarkshire man called Thompson arrived at the test centre and sounded the horn of his car to let the examiner know he was there. The examiner came to the vehicle and informed Thompson, a motor mechanic, that it was illegal to sound the horn while the car was stationary. Thompson failed the test.

The quick and the dead

In 1997 a driver from Miami, Florida, managed to drive several miles without realizing he had a corpse alongside him.

Alvin Sims, aged 36, kept on driving after his 29-year-old girlfriend's head had slammed into a roadside pole. She died instantly.

Sims told police that Donna Richardson had been hanging her head out of the window of his 1993 Chevrolet to be sick. He said he'd been looking for a hospital.

When the accident happened he thought he'd hit a puddle and didn't notice that he'd killed her.

Three times unlucky

Like a kid with a new toy, a chap in Smyrna in the USA bought a shiny new motorbike and invited a friend round to see it.

Unused to motorcycles, he cranked up the engine and the machine shot through a sliding glass door, injuring the new owner, who was dragged with it.

An ambulance took him to hospital while his wife mopped up the spilled petrol and threw the tissue paper down the toilet.

When the would-be motorcyclist returned, heavily bandaged, he went into the toilet and while there lit a cigarette. He smoked, reflecting on his misfortune, and then dropped the dog end down the loo – causing the discarded petrol to explode and throw him against the door, according to a local paper.

So the ambulance was called again and he was put on a stretcher, face down because of his new injuries. Just as his wife was telling him that nothing else could possible go wrong, one of the ambulance men tripped over the motorbike and the patient fell to the floor, injuring his leg.

He didn't go in for motorbikes after that. If only he'd bothered to learn how to use it . . .

Key to disaster

Most men's cars are more important than their spouses, their houses – even their own lives, it seems.

According to press reports a 41-year-old driver in Detroit got stuck and drowned in just two feet (60 centimetres) of water. He had squeezed head first through a hole just eighteen inches (45 centimetres) wide in order to retrieve his car keys from a sewer gate.

The walk home would have been better for him.

Bomb proof

Security guards can be pretty stupid men sometimes. In 1978 security became worried that ground staff were nicking miniature bottles of whisky from a Pan-Am plane, and rigged up a cuckoo clock in the drinks cabinet that would stop if the door was opened, thus showing the time of the theft.

But a particularly stupid person forgot to tell the crew, and a stewardess, Susan Becker, assumed the clock was a bomb. The pilot was alerted and he made an emergency landing at Berlin, passengers scurrying out of the aircraft's fire exits.

Blue moon

The occupants of a small plane were amazed to find three pairs of buttocks pressed against the windows of a passing plane as they were flying over Brazil. What the guys in the other plane were doing was mooning – but they lost control of their craft and it crashed.

They were all found dead in the wreckage with their trousers around their ankles.

Peake of idiocy

The British writer of the weird and wonderful, Mervyn Peake – author of *Gormenghast*, *Titus Groan* and *Titus Alone* – was travelling home to England at the age of 11 on the Trans-Siberian Railway when the train stopped to refuel in the middle of a thousand square miles of desolation.

His older brother Leslie decided he'd like to watch the engineer at work, and got off the train. However, so engrossed was he that he failed to notice when the train began to move off. As it picked up speed, Leslie was left behind, with the prospect of facing an icy wilderness and wolves. It was only at the last moment that his father grabbed his arm and hauled him aboard.

Car that went like a bomb

A New Jersey man was playing with fire when he and his wife decided to try an experiment with a quarter-stick of dynamite. Paul Stiller (47) and his wife Bonnie were in their car at the time, driving around at 2 a.m. in Andover Township.

They decided they'd toss the dynamite out of the window to see what would happen. But neither of them had spotted that the window was closed at the time, and the dynamite bounced right back again.

They were both injured, and Paul needed hospital treatment.

Ticket collector . . .

The most stupid driver must be the man from Frisco in Texas, who managed to break the record for the largest number of traffic offences in the shortest time.

He had hitch-hiked to a nearby city in October 1966 and bought a 1953 Ford. He drove away from the showroom at 3.50 in the afternoon.

Four minutes later he hit a 1952 Chevrolet, and a minute later he collided with another Chevrolet on a street corner.

However, he began to feel more confident and promptly drove the wrong way along a one-way street. Then he hit a Ford.

By the time a further ten minutes had passed, he had been handed ten traffic tickets, hit four cars without stopping, driven four times on the wrong side of the road and caused six accidents.

Sleeping on the sleepers

Chrisoph Fuchs was pretty drunk one night when he wandered on to a railway line in Germany and promptly fell asleep.

The 20-year-old was run over by a train – but suffered no more than a scraped elbow. And he didn't even know about that till he woke up. The driver had spotted him and tried to stop, but couldn't apply the brakes in time.

Fortunately for Fuchs – from Altenglan in the Rheinland – he was lying between the lines and the train went right over him. He told local papers, 'I don't know how I got there. I didn't notice anything.'

Plain loco

There's a book on locomotive design that has a none too complimentary index entry for one Francis Webb, a locomotive designer for the London and North-Western Railway. It says, 'Webb, Francis: his incompetence'. On his Teutonic class of locos he had two pairs of driving wheels that weren't connected and could go in opposite directions at the same time. So the trains wouldn't budge.

One way of going nowhere fast.

Botany stray

A pioneer botanist called Thomas Nuttall (1786–1859) was an expert at getting lost – usually in parts of north-west America. His colleagues often had to light beacons during one expedition in 1812, in order to help him to get back to camp.

One night they had to search for him, but as they approached where he was he thought they were Indians and made a dash for it, leaving his would-be rescuers pursuing him for three days. Then he just nonchalantly wandered back into camp.

Fly away, Peter

Sir Peter Parker, chairman of what used to be called British Rail, was on his way to a meeting with Cumbria County Council in July 1978, but he got on the wrong train at Crewe. He realized his mistake and had to wrap a note around a coin and toss it out of the window as the train passed through Tamworth station in Staffordshire. The note said, 'Please apologize to Cumbria Council and tell them I won't be able to make it.' He got to London and set off again – by aeroplane.

THE WORLD OF ENTERTAINMENT

Entertainers can sometimes be so . . . well, entertaining. And sometimes they don't even have to try. Take the case of the actor who forgot just about everything, or the hypnotist who decided it wasn't necessary to *see* in order to drive a car in a city street.

And now for something completely different

The Times called it 'memory loss on a grand scale' when Paul Greenwood, an actor, forgot most of his lines – and moves – in a production of *The Happiest Days of Your Life* at the Barbican on 24 July 1984.

It all started because he was supposed to make a note, but had no lead in his propelling pencil. Then he discovered he had no ink in his biro. This must have had a distracting effect on him, because from then on he was flustered, and after a few correct lines launched into several that his fellow players just didn't recognize.

They recognized the lines he began to utter in Act II, however: they were theirs, not his. Eventually, Greenwood turned to the audience and said, 'I'm sorry, we'll have to stop because I'm talking nonsense up here. You see, there was no lead in my pencil.' (A wag of a fellow actor remarked that this had always been his problem.)

And so to Act III, where Greenwood forgot the plot and at one point asked the audience, 'Shall I start again?' They all roared in the affirmative.

One critic reviewed the performance of the prompter.

Watch this space

It couldn't have happened at a more inopportune moment. There was Professor James Gaddarn, of Trinity College of Music, London, ready to conduct Ealing Choral Society and Orchestra in the last movement of Beethoven's *Missa Solemnis*.

Then the professor – who had his back to the audience – heard a commotion and, on looking round, saw a spaceman complete with silver helmet and big boots.

Gaddarn asked him, 'What do you want?' but could hear only mumbles from the helmet.

However, the professor was eventually able to ascertain that the strange apparition was from a kissogram agency – and he'd come to the wrong hall.

Auntie's bloomers

Even the good old BBC cocks up now and again, and did so spectacularly in 1944 when King Haakon VII of Norway, in exile from his Nazi-occupied country, gave a rousing wartime address to his people on the World Service. But he was running about forty seconds short, so a producer nipped off for a sound effect.

Haakon was coming to the end of his talk. He commended his country to God, said a few Nordic farewells and put down his script.

Then the airwaves burst into the unmistakable sounds of Cockneys shouting, 'Roll up, roll up, ladies and gentlemen.' This was accompanied by the sound of roundabouts and other fairground attractions.

The producer had taken the wrong FX tape.

Carmen to get you . . .

At Heidelberg in Germany the rapt audience during Bizet's *Carmen* were not aware that a real-life drama was about to take place – all because the performer playing Don José had forgotten to bring on stage his prop knife, with which he was supposed to stab Carmen.

Thinking quickly – if not altogether sensibly – he decided to strangle her instead.

He put his hands around the unfortunate – and unsuspecting – woman's throat and she thought he'd gone quite mad, and so fought back fiercely.

She kept on singing, though – even though the critics said she was sounding a bit muffled.

Blind test

The hypnotist Romark decided he'd like to try a rather unusual test of his powers and duly announced in 1977 that he would drive a car, blindfold, through Ilford. In October that year he put two coins and a slice of dough across his eyes, held with a thick band, and set off down Cranbrook Road in his Renault.

He had gone but twenty yards when he drove into the back of a parked police van. Romark declared, 'That van was parked in a place that logic told me it wouldn't be.'

Definitely not a winner

Mike Stacey was a crook on the run – and you'd think he'd stay out of the limelight. Not Mike. He was spotted by US cops as he appeared in the American version of *Who Wants To Be a Millionaire?* But as soon as he stepped out of the studio he was arrested.

Police said, 'He was in the wrong place at the wrong time – plus he didn't win any money.'

Another person rooting for his capture was Holly Carr, a clerk at the court where Stacey – aged 31 at the time – owed the equivalent of £10,000 in fines for selling counterfeit T-shirts. Carr said, 'He owes this court so much money, we were hoping he'd win some.'

Act of remorse

In April 2000 a TV station in Rome reported the tragic outcome of a young man's desire to create an authentic death scene for Judas Iscariot in a religious play.

Most actors would have used a non-working noose, but not this 23-year-old thespian. As Judas, consumed with remorse for having betrayed Jesus, he went off and stood on a rock with the noose around his neck. But he slipped and the noose tightened, asphyxiating him.

The incident happened during an outdoor drama in Camerata Nuova, a hamlet of 200 people about 45 miles from Rome.

The regional TV station – RAI TV – showed an amateur video that captured the screams and reactions of actors and audience when they realized that Renato di Paolo wasn't acting but was unconscious.

He was dead on arrival at hospital.

Genoa good joke?

In his wonderful book *The Return of Heroic Failures* (Martin Secker and Warburg Ltd, 1988), Stephen Pile reproduces the English programme notes for the

Genoa Opera Company's production of Bizet's *Carmen* in 1981. Who was the more stupid, the translator, or the administrators for letting him anywhere near the programme, is anyone's guess. However, the notes are definitely worth reproducing here:

ACT ONE: Carmen, a cigarmakeress from a tobago factory, loves Don Jose of the mounting guard. Carmen takes a flower from her corsets and lances it to Don Jose. (Duet: 'Talk me of my mother.') There was noise inside the tobago factory and revolting cigarmakeresses burst onto the stage. Carmen is arrested and Don Jose is ordered to mounting guard on her but she subduces him and lets her escape.

ACT TWO: The Tavern. Carmen sings (Aria: 'The sistrums tinkling.') Enter two smugglers ('Ho, we have in mind a business.') Enter Escamillio, a Balls fighter. Carmen refuses to penetrate because Don Jose has liberated her from prison. He just now arrives. (Aria: 'Slop here who comes.') But here are the bugles singing his retreat. Don Jose will leave and draws his sword. Called by Carmen's shrieks the two smugglers interfere with her. Jose is bound to dessert. Final Chorus: 'Opening Sky Wandering Life.'

ACT THREE: A rocky landscape. Smugglers chatter. Carmen sees her death in the cards. Don Jose makes a date with her for the next Balls fight.

ACT FOUR: A Place in Seville. Procession of Ballfighters. The roaring of Balls is heard in the arena. Escamillio enters (Aria and Chorus: 'Toreador. Toreador. All hail the Balls of a toreador.') Enter Don Jose (Aria: 'I besmooch you.') Carmen repels him. She wants to join with Escamillio now chaired by the crowd. Don Jose stabbs her. (Aria: 'Oh, rupture, rupture.') He sings: 'Oh, my subductive Carmen.'

Noteworthy performance

This entry is a tribute to the technicians at a 1970s orchestral concert in the USA, where Tchaikovsky's *1812* Overture was being played. That's the one with a particularly noisy finale, complete with cannons and bells. As the finale came close, the electrical firing system that would have set off the cannons one by one failed, and all sixteen went off together. This not only spoiled the finale – although the orchestra played on – but set off the smoke alarms.

So the overture's climax had not only a huge boom from the cannons, but fire bells, smoke alarms, some klaxons and hooters and a shower of safety foam from the automatic sprinklers. Then there was the braying of the sirens as six fire engines arrived.

The kindest cut of all . . .?

The South Koreans liked *The Sound of Music*, but not the . . . well, the music part. And, because the film was a bit overlong for their tastes, they decided to shorten it a bit. Which they did – by taking out all the songs.

They still called it *The Sound of Music*, and it played to full houses all over South-East Asia. You know, maybe this entry doesn't really qualify for inclusion in a book about *stupid* things men do, after all . . .

What goes down . . .

Sword swallowing has always been an attraction at circuses and the like. And the swords are actually swallowed: it's not a trick. The secret is to keep the oesophagus – the food pipe – nice and straight and keep still. Oh, and don't try to sing, talk, cough or sneeze.

However, a German sword swallower decided to go one further in the cause of spectacle and used an umbrella. Unfortunately, it was one of those automatic things with a little button that you press to . . .

Yes, you've guessed it.

A TASTE OF FUNNY

Nothing is immune to the stupidity of men, it seems – not even food and drink. There was the chap who wanted to make his drink a little stronger and ended up burning his house down; and then there was the diner who sexually assaulted the fiddler in the fancy restaurant.

Foot-loose

In Tacoma, Washington State, Kerry Bingham had been drinking with friends and the conversation got around to bungee jumping. As more drink was consumed, Bingham and nine other men trooped along the walkway of the Tacoma Narrows Bridge in the middle of traffic intending to bungee-jump. However, no one had brought any bungee rope.

Bingham had drunk more than the rest, and volunteered to use a coil of lineman's cable that lay near by. One end was secured around his leg and the other to the bridge.

Bingham fell forty feet before the cable tightened

and pulled off his foot at the ankle. He survived the fall into the icy river and was rescued by two fishermen.

Bet he was swimming round in circles, though.

Good night, sweet prince!

Derek Davies was Third Secretary at the British Embassy in Vienna in 1960 and went to a fancy-dress party attired as Hamlet. Lovely costume: satin blouse, pair of gorgeous tights and a wig. His Yorick was a Burmese tiger's skull with an ashtray set into it along with a receptacle for matches.

The party went well, but it was getting colder outside, and when Davies went to his Morris Minor it was entombed in snow. There were no matches left in the receptacle in the Yorick skull, so – perhaps not thinking too straight after imbibing – he put his lips to the lock and tried to defrost it with his breath. Unfortunately, his lips became stuck to the lock because of the frost on the metal door. He couldn't shout: all he *could* do was wave the skull frantically in the hope of being seen.

When he was eventually rescued by two Viennese policeman who were confronted by this man in colourful tights and a wig, bending over, kissing a car door and waving a tiger's skull in the air, they were at a loss as to what to be most astounded by.

Waiter, there's a fly on my tenner

Diners in a fashionable King's Road restaurant in London looked on with hilarity and amazement as a diner began to get friendly with a musician.

The violinist was employed to serenade the customers, as he moved between the tables. One particular diner – a member of a party – saw that the violinist's actions were causing embarrassment to a woman in the group, and so he tried to tip the performer ten quid as a heavy hint for him to move on. He leaned back and tried to shove the ten-pound note into the violinist's pocket.

And this was when the hilarity began – for the diner was trying to push the banknote into the fiddler's fly.

Drop of the hard stuff

A young man from Canada was looking for a cheap way to get drunk because he was broke and couldn't afford booze. So he mixed some petrol with milk. As you would expect, he felt a little ill after imbibing this concoction and threw up into the fireplace of his house.

The petrol in his vomit exploded on contact with the fire and his house burned down – killing both him and his sister.

Loss of face

A man at a party in Kincaid, West Virginia, put a blasting cap into his mouth and bit down on it, triggering an explosion that blew off his lips, teeth and tongue.

Twenty-four-year-old Jerry Stromyer of Kincaid did it as a prank.

Corporal M. D. Payne of the Kincaid Police Department said, 'Another man had it in an aquarium, hooked to a battery, and was trying to explode it. It wouldn't go off and this guy said, ' "I'll show you how to set it off." He put it in his mouth and bit down. It blew all his teeth off, his tongue and his lips.'

A spokesman for the Charleston Area Medical Division said, 'I just can't imagine anyone doing something like that.'

STUPIDITY
WITH A BANG

Most men are stupid most of the time. Give a guy a
gun and he's off his trolley, out of his tree, an
incomplete shilling – plumb crazy. Like the man
who played Russian roulette with the seriously *wrong*
sort of gun. Or the student who lost part of his man-
hood with a bang – and probably ensured that his
sex life wouldn't go with one.

Cock-sure

In December 1999 a student at the University of
Michigan was playing with a gun – as so many
North Americans are wont to do – and shot off part
of his penis.

He was stripped to boxer shorts at the time, for
reasons that are not clear, and the gun went off. He
needed emergency surgery.

The incident was apparently a 'pledge', or dare,
within his fraternity.

Assured defeat

A 19-year-old man from Houston in Texas decided in February 2000 that he fancied a game of Russian roulette. So he took his handgun to visit friends and told them what he planned to do.

What he didn't realize was that his .45 semiautomatic pistol was just that – a semiautomatic pistol. Unlike a revolver, which in Russian roulette has five of its six chambers empty, it automatically inserts a round into the firing chamber when the gun is cocked, however many rounds have been removed from the magazine.

He lost the game by shooting himself dead.

Doggone it!

A man in Port St John, Florida, had malevolent intentions towards a neighbour's dog in November 1999 as he stood in his front garden aiming a gun at the animal.

Unfortunately for him, he was pointing the gun at his own foot when he pulled the trigger, putting him in hospital.

According to *Florida Today*, he wasn't much liked by his neighbours anyway, so his failed attempt to harm man's best friend was greeted with some amusement.

POTTY PROJECTS

Images of absent-minded professors and enthusiastic amateurs with their hair on fire or their faces blackened come to mind when we think of inventors. And they can be pretty innovative in providing us with some laughs, like the chap who went to work on an egg, or the guy who came up with the tasty ultimate in religious icons.

On yer bike, Arthur

'A bicycle with amphibious capacity' was just one of 162 patented inventions – none of them successful – of one Arthur Paul Pedrick. He patented his innovations between 1962 and 1977. Another was a pair of glasses that improved vision in bad visibility.

Pedrick described himself as the 'One-Man Think-Tank Basic Physics Research Laboratories' of Selsey in Sussex, and one grand scheme he thought of was to irrigate desert regions by sending snowballs from the polar regions through a chain of giant peashooters.

If that first shot off the tee is your weak point on the golf course, you may be interested in one of his golf inventions: it was a golf ball that could be steered in flight. Unfortunately, it was against the rules.

My Sweet Lord

An Australian confectioner who wanted to put some spirituality back into Easter decided to invent the 'Sweet Jesus' chocolate. It was a crucifix with a Christ figure on it, which bled red jelly when bitten into.

Wouldn't it be in bad taste for those of a religious disposition? Not at all, said the Canberra producer of the sweetmeat. 'The object,' he said, 'is to put religion back into Easter with an edible icon. People who are offended by the icon have lost touch with reality. A Sweet Jesus crucifix will remind them that Easter is more than three days on the beach.'

Flight of fancy

Believe it or not, the world's first crashproof aeroplane looked like a metal egg with prongs. A French inventor called Sauvant claimed in 1932 that this unlikely contraption could crash and anyone inside would escape unscathed.

His reasoning was that, according to his experiments, if a hen's egg is placed inside a larger ostrich's egg, the embryo in the smaller egg would be unaffected by damage to the larger. One newspaper said, 'No explanation of how the smaller egg is placed inside the larger one has yet appeared, nor have we been told what fate befalls the ostrich.'

Local gendarmes didn't quite believe him and on three occasions confiscated the wheels of his contraption to he couldn't take off. Not to be outmanoeuvred by the law, Sauvant decided to ask some friends to push him off an eight-foot cliff in Nice.

But he didn't so much fly as plummet, and his friends looked down to see him amid the wreckage of his 'plane' looking decidedly dazed. However, he was to declare later that he was delighted that the experiment had been such a success.

LAW AND DISORDER

We love crime. The statistics prove it. We watch more crime movies and read more crime novels than any other genre. Actually, I've just made that up – but I bet it's a fact.

What's behind our obsession with it? Dunno, but it's certainly good for a laugh, whether it's an Ealing comedy or this section of *Stupid Things Men Do*.

Terrible terrorists

The Gatti Gang were about the most stupid terrorists you could imagine. This Milan-based mob – a cell of Italy's Red Brigade – had had only one bomb during the course of their existence, and they were so frightened of it that a fellow terrorist told them, 'Give up. You're a danger to everyone.'

The gang's robberies were no more successful. For one thing, none of them could drive, so they had to go by bus – or occasionally on a motor scooter. Their most successful hold-up netted them about 18,000 lire (then worth around £9).

They were also too stupid to look after their hardware: all their handguns were too rusty to work. While trying to get new ones on one occasion they were swindled out of £1,000 in an arms deal that went wrong.

Eventually, their leader, Enrico Gatti, gave himself up and urged the other 27 members to do the same.

How not to commit robbery in several easy lessons

In February 1990 in the Renton area of Seattle a man who seemed to have little experience of the art of holding up stores decided to do just that. But he made several fatal errors:

He chose the wrong target. It was a firearms shop, and it was full of customers. And this was in a state where many people are licensed to carry guns concealed on their person.

In order to get into the shop he had to step around a King County police patrol car parked right outside the front door.

Inside, a cop in uniform was standing chatting over the counter, having a coffee before going on duty.

When he saw the officer, the would-be robber announced he was holding up the store, and began firing rounds at random, whereupon the officer and a shop assistant returned fire, killing him.

Piano — and forte

A Soviet housebreaker at Baku on the Caspian Sea entered a flat while the owners were on holiday, and began a thorough looting of the premises. However, at the end of it he was exhausted, so he ran himself a hot bath, and after he'd dried off sat down and knocked back a couple of vodkas.

He then poured himself another, and took a stroll to the upright piano in the room, and began to play Grieg's piano concerto.

He'd got the *animato* section and was loudly singing along (singing without words, presumably, since the piece doesn't have any) when the police arrived, having been alerted by complaining neighbours who didn't like the noise.

Banging away

The three Danish crooks had worked all day trying to dynamite open the safe at the bank in Munkebo. They tried six times the required amount of dynamite but the safe would not open.

But so hard had they tried that they managed to demolish the bank in an explosion that could be heard ten miles away.

No thought for the neighbours, of course.

Bombed out

A would-be bomber in Iraq wanted to send a very special parcel – of a rather explosive kind. Unfortunately, he didn't put enough postage on the package and it came back to him with a stamp saying 'Return to sender'.

Unfortunately, he had not remembered that it was his parcel bomb and he opened it. The inevitable happened. He didn't survive to tell the tale.

Hands off!

A chap from Brentford was fined £2 for riding his bicycle carelessly. He had been riding with his hands off the handlebars and gripping a newspaper, which he was reading at the time.

'It's the only chance I ever get to read the newspaper,' he told the magistrates.

Caught napping

In the French village of Lachelle in 1964, a Parisian burglar broke into a house but immediately began to feel peckish. So he found the fridge and helped himself to some of his favourite cheese. Still not sated, he extended his search until he found some Bath Oliver biscuits.

But it was the champagne that was his downfall.

He found three bottles and quaffed the lot, leading to a distinct feeling of drowsiness.

So off he went in search of a spare bedroom – where he was found the next morning and promptly arrested.

Downtime

When bank robbers in Los Angeles brandished their shotguns and yelled to everyone to get down on the floor, they didn't realize how literally all the bank's occupants would take it.

Bank clerks, security guards and customers all dropped to the floor and lay prostrate, fearing for their lives. Problem was that there was no one to fill the crooks' bag with loot.

They stood for a while, looking somewhat confused and bewildered, and then left.

Get me outta here!

In 1982 a burglar decided to try his luck in one of the palatial mansions in Millionaire's Row in Bel Air, LA. Equipped with a sack and his breaking-in tools, off he went, intending to nip smartly through the house while the owners were asleep, collecting goodies along the way.

Once in, he went through the ballroom and into the hall and down an escalator. He found himself in the swimming arbour. Then he went up to the library and across the dining room, out of the annexe and into a conservatory, where he found he was the object of the attention of a cageful of parrots.

Having collected enough stuff, he decided it was time to leave. So he went back through the dining room and up to the gym, across the indoor tennis court and down a winding staircase, at the bottom of which he found he was in an enclosed patio with fountains. So he went out to the cocktail lounge, through what he took to be the son's soundproofed drum studio, and back into the room with the parrots.

So he ran back towards the library, and through swing doors into a gallery of paintings. Panicking by now, he ran out through the kitchen and across a Jacuzzi enclosure, then up two flights of stairs, outside along the balcony and around a circular corridor, before finding more stairs. Then he was going down on to a landing and, hysterical by now, he went into the master bedroom and asked the startled occupants how he could get out.

They arranged for the local police department to oblige.

Hey, I'm over here!

A weekly aviation newsletter in the USA, AVweb, reported that a burglar had broken into a Mooney aircraft at the airport at Knox, Ohio, and removed its avionics system.

This had included the ELT (emergency locating transmitter), which is a device that sends out homing signals if the aircraft crashes.

You've probably realized by now what happened. Yes, the bungling burglar activated the device and was easily traced by the authorities.

Dear Sir, I am going to kill you

Representative Jim Kaster of Texas once introduced a Bill that would require anybody intending to commit a crime to tell their future victim at least 24 hours before the event. Oh, and potential victims must notify would-be perpetrators of their right to use deadly force to ward off said crime.

Funny money

A 22-year-old man in Wichita was arrested for trying to pass off two counterfeit banknotes at a hotel. It wasn't that the ink was the wrong colour, or that they were the wrong size, or printed on material that didn't feel right: they were $16 bills.

Hush my mouth!

Honesty was definitely not the best policy for an Oklahoma man charged with armed robbery of a shop. He decided he'd represent himself in court and all was going well until the shop manager went on to the witness stand.

She was asked, 'Can you identify the man who held up your store?'

She replied, pointing to the defendant, 'That's him.' At that the defendant jumped to his feet, told her she was lying, and cried, 'I should've blown your fucking head off!'

There was a quick pause before he added, 'If I'd been the one that was there.'

Headlight

According to newspaper reports, a burglar was doing a job in a bicycle shop in Lompoc, California, and fell through the ceiling. Unfortunately, 24-year-old Santiago Alvarado had been holding the torch he was using in his mouth to free his hands for use in carrying out his nefarious intentions.

Such a fall would not normally be fatal, but the torch rammed into his skull when he hit the floor.

The Italian job

The crooks had got it right to the last second. Perfect timing. They had planned the raid on a bank at Artema, near Rome, in February 1980 down to the last detail. However, they didn't know the bank had closed three minutes early because things had gone a bit quiet, and the gang leader managed to run straight into a plate-glass door – now locked – and knocked himself unconscious.

He was bundled by his accomplices into the waiting getaway car and driven away. Empty-handed.

Have no gun, will travel . . .

There's nothing like going well equipped for the job. And this was *nothing* like going well equipped for the job.

The would-be robber who tried to hold up Mohammed Razaq's grocery shop in Wandsworth in July 1979 spat out his threat: 'Give me the money from your till or I'll shoot!'

Mr Razaq, though, kept cool and, in a moment that exemplified his accustomed eye for detail, asked, 'Where is your gun?'

The intruder was obliged to say that he did not, after all, have a gun. But if Mr Razaq wanted to be difficult about it he would go out, get one and come back. So there.

Whereupon he left, and was not seen again.

Lies, damned lies and photocopiers

Police in Radnor, Pennsylvania, had a novel way to make the suspect cough up. They put a metal colander on his head and connected it with wires to a photocopier in which a piece of paper bearing the words 'HE'S LYING' had been placed.

Each time they thought he wasn't telling the truth they pressed the copy button, and out came a copy saying, 'He's lying.'

The stupid suspect believed the device was a genuine lie detector, and confessed his crime.

It's a fair cop

A robber in Ionia, Michigan, was so drunk when he tried to demand money from two garage attendants that when they refused to hand over the cash, he threatened to call the police.

And, after they had refused a second time, that was just what he did. The police arrived and promptly arrested him.

One-way ticket

It couldn't be easier, thought the bank robber in Malta when he decided to hold up the Bank of Valetta. He rounded up the staff at gunpoint and seized the cash. Then he rushed out of the bank and dashed across the road.

To the bus stop.

Where he waited for fifteen minutes – with no sign of a bus.

He was arrested by a passing policeman, who was just a mite suspicious when he clapped eyes on the 3,000 new banknotes the man was holding to his chest.

Typical, though, isn't it? You wait fifteen minutes for a bus and then a cop turns up!

More equal than others . . .

The European Economic Community – as it was then known – told the Irish government in 1976 that it should put in place equal-opportunities legislation to ensure equal pay between the sexes. So the government advertised for an officer to enforce the equal-pay policy. Trouble was, the ad offered different salary scales for men and women . . .

Slippery customer

When Christopher Fleming went a-burgling in 1978 he thought the job at the Chinese restaurant would be simple. Just nip in via the kitchen window, take as many notes as possible from the till and get out through the same window.

But he lost his balance and fell into a chip fryer, getting himself covered in grease. Undaunted, he clambered out and went to the till, only to find there were no notes in it at all.

So he grabbed as much loose change as he could – amounting to about £20 – and with his greasy overcoat well and truly congealed he walked out of the restaurant and into the arms of a policeman.

Judge not, that ye be not judged

The judge was really asking for it. Lord Birkenhead, when he was F. E. Smith, a barrister, referred to one of the witnesses as being 'as drunk as a judge' at the time of an offence. The learned judge looked over his spectacles at the bewigged Smith and informed him that in his learned opinion the accustomed saying was 'drunk as a lord'.

'As Your Lordship pleases,' came the witty riposte.

Returning to the scene of the crime

Two crooks from Edmonton in Canada decided to hold up a petrol station in Vancouver.

They bustled the attendant into the toilet, locked him in and made off with a hundred dollars. But then they got lost. Having driven around for a while, they came across a petrol station and decided to ask directions.

But it was the same gas station they'd robbed. And they didn't recognize the attendant, because, in the struggle to get him into the toilet, they hadn't seen much of his face.

The attendant decided to play it cool and gave them directions, and, as soon as they began walking away, called the police.

Then the two guys came back another time and asked for a mechanic. The attendant – still playing things cool – said there wouldn't be a mechanic on till 8 a.m. the following day.

The police arrived as the robbers were trying to phone for a tow truck.

Safe bet

A gang in Chichester broke into the Southern Leisure Centre to crack open the safe. They were using the latest, state-of-the-art cutting gear – but managed only to weld the safe's door up.

The manager said afterwards that the safe was more secure for the efforts of the would-be thieves, and it had taken three hours to break it open using a hammer and chisel.

Taxi!

The Danish bank robber was pretty proud of his progress so far. He'd held up the bank and had in his hand a sackful of money. All he needed to do was dash outside and hail a taxi. Seeing a car with a light on top, he jumped in with his booty and shouted out his home address.

But it was a police car.

DANGER: MEN AT WORK

If I might essay a variation on that well-known law of C. Northcote Parkinson that says, 'Work expands so as to fill the time available for its completion', I'd say stupidity expands to accommodate all the kinds of work that can be done by men.

Take the chaps who pulled the plug out of the canal and let all the water out, or the DIY enthusiast who should have been put out of everyone's misery.

A jet-black day

In 1987 the US Navy launched an inquiry to find the identity of a mechanic at Jacksonville Air Depot whose stupidity led to the grounding of 300 jets.

A Navy spokesman told reporters, 'We were told he was simply not mechanically inclined. For years this guy was taking these gearboxes apart, then putting them back together – with parts left over when he was done.'

Fortunately, there were no serious accidents, although there were technical hitches, and the Navy sent teams worldwide with a bulletin ordering anyone flying these aircraft to see if a job had been signed 'Wood' or 'Woods', or with an illegible mark.

The planes that were affected were the A-4 Skyhawk, the EA-6B Prowler electronic-warfare plane and the A-6 Intruder attack plane.

Bombed out

Carpenters working on a house in the Philippines in December 1998 managed to kill the owner and three other people after they'd uncovered an unexploded World War Two bomb.

The carpenters were installing a septic tank at the house in Tacloban, 360 miles south-east of Manila, when they found the bomb – but left it around for *fifteen days*. Then they decided to tinker with it. When someone tinkers with an unexploded bomb there's a possibility that it might just go off. This one did.

A Fishy tale!

I hesitate to call that nice Mr Fish stupid, but he was probably feeling a bit that way after his disastrous weather forecast in October 1987.

Michael Fish – one of Britain's best-known TV and radio weather forecasters – told viewers that 'a woman rang to say she'd heard there was a hurricane on the way. Well, don't worry. There isn't.'

He gave a chuckle and went on to predict 'a showery airflow' and some 'sea breezes'.

But very soon the country was assailed by 120-mile-an-hour winds that tore up 300 miles of power cables, blocked 200 roads with fallen branches and trees, tore down a quarter of the trees in Kent, stopped all rail traffic in the south of England and cut off power to a quarter of the country – and all in 24 hours. The Met Office announced that it was the worst hurricane since 1703. But of Fish a spokesman could say only that it was 'really all a question of detail'.

Asleep on high

A baggage handler at London's Heathrow Airport was in the hold of a Tri-Star, and decided he needed a rest as he waited for the last bag to come aboard. So he lay down and the inevitable happened: he fell asleep.

When he awoke the plane was in the air. The flight crew responded to his cries for help and he was freed via a trapdoor leading from the hold into the toilet. He was taken to a seat and given a hot meal.

However, when the plane landed in Bermuda, he was put on the first flight back home by immigration officials. Not only did his workmates take the mickey once he was home, but British Airways billed him £298 for the flight!

Desperate Dan

Stupid or just unlucky? Maybe a bit of both. But the exploits of Dan Raschen are to be found in a book whose title says it all: *Wrong Again, Dan!*
Among his misadventures are:

- As he was bound for India to join his regiment in 1944 he lost his underwear and his only pair of pyjamas while washing them out of a porthole.
- He lost the ship's cutlery when he threw out a bowl of dishwater with the cutlery still in it. The troops on board had to eat with their fingers for the rest of the voyage.
- When he arrived he was accused of murder – only to be able to point out the supposed victim of this dastardly deed standing in a crowd, grinning.
- He was put in charge of three amphibious tanks – but managed to lose them all: two in a pond, where they'd got stuck, and one that went through the wall of his own accommodation.
- He decided to go into explosives and one day tried to blow up some coral reef. But he'd moored his own boat to the reef that was receiving his attention, with the inevitable consequences.

Dan's book was published by Buckland Press of London.

Danger! Man at work!

Antony Drew of Kent must go down as one of the most 'interesting' DIY experts of all time with this catalogue of calamity. First he wanted to put up a new shower curtain, and took his ladder into the bathroom but managed with consummate ease to fall off it and splinter the enamel in the bath, while his hammer cracked the bath itself. The drill, meanwhile, which had also been tossed into the air as Drew fell, smashed the washbasin.

Not to be deterred, off went Mr Drew to repair the fireplace – but managed to stick his hammer through the television screen.

So it was back to the ladder. He took it outside and climbed up to the bathroom window to paint it. Whether it was something to do with bathrooms or ladders – or the combination of the two – we'll never know. But he managed to fall off it again, sending his chisel flying through the window and himself crashing through the carport.

Bottom secret

A Soviet spy called R. E. de Bruyeker must have felt pretty stupid when he gave the enemy all they needed to track him down.

He'd broken into the NATO naval base at Agnano, near Naples, while spying for the Soviets in 1976, and stole a box of top-secret files.

But he managed to leave behind his overnight bag, which had a copy of *Playboy* in it as well as details about himself and his planned movements. He was traced immediately, of course.

Canal capers

Workmen were busy on the Chesterfield–Stockwith Canal in England in 1978. They'd been tasked with moving all the old prams and bike wheels and other detritus that had accumulated over the years.

As they worked, a policeman arrived during the workmen's extended lunch break to say he was investigating a giant whirlpool in the canal some-where upriver. The workmen went back to the canal and could see no whirlpool, but could see what had caused it. The water had gone. There was just a length of mud – dotted with all the old prams and bits of old bike.

What they hadn't realized was that one of the first things they'd hauled out of the water had been the plug that had for the past two hundred years kept the water in the canal. 'We didn't know there was a plug,' one workmen was reported as saying. The records covering the canal had been lost during a wartime fire, so no one had known the details of its structure.

Needless to say, the workmen got a number of complaints from irate holidaymakers whose boats had become stranded on the mud.

Destroyers destroyed

The Luftwaffe bomber pilot must have felt pretty proud of himself on 22 February 1940 as he flew off the coast of the German island of Borkum. There he saw two destroyers, and gave them all he'd got, doing more damage than any one plane had done before.

Unfortunately, the destroyers, the *Lebrecht Maass* and the *Max Schultz*, both belonged to the German Navy.

Going down . . .

A keen DIY enthusiast in Gloucester, Michael Taylor, decided he'd like an extra room. So he decided to lower the floor of his cellar.

Unfortunately, he dug at the foundations till the entire building collapsed.

Hay, take a look at this!

It was one of the most exciting archaeological finds of the century, or so thought a team of researchers in Tehran.

They'd uncovered a very special skeleton – that of a dinosaur that had so far been found only in North America. The vertebrae and ribs were handled with the utmost care, and a team of scientists flew out in 1930 to conduct a rigid analysis of the 'find' – only to find that the 'reptile' was a haymaking machine that had been abandoned after having been caught in a landslide.

Oh, Mr Porter!

Henry Porter, a distinguished British journalist, told his *Sunday Times* readers in May 1986 that he had planted five deliberate grammatical errors in his column that day. He offered to send a bottle of champagne to anyone who spotted them all.

No one did. But letters came by the sackful, nevertheless. Readers had found a further 23 errors of which Porter was not aware.

Here to stay

You've heard of painting yourself into a corner? Well, there were these workmen in Otley in Yorkshire who had the job in 1979 of erecting a fence at the Bennett Court old-folk's home so the residents would have more privacy.

The workmen duly arrived and got down to the job, assiduously sinking the posts and erecting a fence three and a half feet (1 metre) high, and a hundred yards (91 metres) long altogether. However, they'd forgotten to leave a gap to get their lorry out.

Elizabeth Whittaker, one of the residents, told a local newspaper, 'It was like watching a Laurel and Hardy film. You could see them looking at the fence, then at the lorry, then at the fence again. Some of us had wondered about the lorry, but we didn't want to interfere.'

A spokesperson for the council told the paper, 'It was an oversight. Maybe they got carried away in their work.' He said the workmen returned the next morning and created a gap by knocking down part of their diligent work, and rescued their incarcerated lorry.

Bulletproof but not idiot-proof

Police in Dahlonega, Georgia, USA, say a cadet called Nick Berrena was stabbed to death in January 1998 by a fellow cadet, Jeffrey Hoffman. Hoffman, aged 23, was trying to prove that a knife could not penetrate the flak vest that 21-year-old Berrena was wearing.

It did.

There was a similar occurrence in Moscow, when a drunk security guard asked a colleague at the Moscow bank they were guarding to stab his bulletproof vest to see how effective it was. It wasn't: the 25-year-old guard died of a heart wound.

Out of the frame

The *Carmel Independent* in California ran a competition for readers to identify from a school photograph which pupil went on to become famous. However, the subeditor whose job it was to lay out the page was overzealous when it came to cropping the picture. He accidentally cut out the pupils who had found stardom, making it impossible for anyone to win the competition.

Plumb crazy!

The Revd Phillip Randall, vicar of Eye near Peterborough, was writing a history of his parish and wanted to include short biographies of some of the local notables of the past. He came upon the initials HWP on a tombstone inside St Matthew's church and set about trying to find who the mysterious HWP might have been. Henry Walter Ponsonby? Harold William Popple? How about Hilary Worthington-Postlethwaite?

Try as he might, he just could not track down the elusive villager, and after a fruitless search that lasted nine years he put a request for help in his parish magazine.

He got his answer when a parishioner rang him to say that the initials HWP stood for 'hot-water pipe'.

Poles apart

Workmen in Ballymacra in County Antrim had a simple enough job to do: they had to take up a telegraph pole and substitute another one. However, there was a slight problem in the shape of a postbox attached to the pole. Because they didn't have the keys to open the clips that held the box to the pole, they simply raised the box to the top and then reversed the process to attach the box to the new pole (this, we assume was before any cables were attached to it!).

But there was a snag: the new pole was a bit thicker, and after much pulling and puffing the box would come only so far down: about nine feet (2.7 metres) above the ground! And there it stayed for three weeks, even though some post managed to get through – thanks to someone's bright idea of placing a stepladder alongside the pole.

Rare to medium stupidity

A nightwatchman in Canada who used microwave energy to keep warm got himself cooked on Christmas morning 1998.

Edward Baker (31) was working for a telephone relay company and was trying to keep warm by using a telecommunications feedhorn. He'd already been suspended once for a breach of safety rules, according to a spokeswoman for Northern Manitoba Signal Relay, Tanya Cooke.

Apparently, Baker got cold on the twelve-hour shifts, during which the temperature would reach 40 below zero.

He didn't realize that microwaves cook from the inside by heating molecules of moisture. He'd taken a twelve-pack of beer and a lawn chair and positioned himself directly in line with the strongest microwave beam.

Perhaps his bosses were just as stupid: they hadn't told him about a tenfold boost in microwave power planned that night to handle an expected increase in holiday long-distance calling traffic.

His body was discovered by the day watchman. His unopened beer cans had exploded.

Post waste . . .

Whoever painted the bin for doggies' doodoos red must be feeling pretty damned stupid. It certainly wasn't appreciated by the good people of Easingwold, near York. The doggie-waste bin should have been green. The result of the unexpected change to the colour scheme was that some people posted their letters in it.

The bin was even mounted on a pole, so it looked even more like a postbox. It had been supplied by a building firm developing a nearby housing estate, and they'd painted it the wrong colour.

Rubble trouble

Solihull Council hired a firm of contractors to knock down some cowsheds on the Stratford Road, near Birmingham, in December 1980. They were badly in need of repair – so much so that they weren't worth repairing.

Off went the contractors one Sunday morning, when eyewitnesses noticed an excavator moving at some speed along the road. It reached the cowsheds, turned off on the wrong side and set out for nearby Monkspath Hall. What the driver didn't know, it seemed, was that Monkspath Hall – set in fields with a lovely tree-lined approach – was a listed eighteenth-century building and thought to be one of the most famous farmhouses in the Midlands.

But it took the chap just three-quarters of an hour to reduce it to a heap of rubble.

Rude mechanical

Donic was a robot and he was bought in 1980 by the enterprising owner of the Kavoi Restaurant in Leith, Scotland, to act as a wine waiter. Unfortunately, the operating instructions had been given to the restaurant's resident disc jockey – who wasn't entirely *au fait* with the intricacies of operating wine-serving automata.

Donic was duly dressed in waiter's garb and looked the part. However, deciding that serving wine was boring, the cybernetic servant thought it would be much more fun to run amuck. Which he did.

Soon tables were smashed and wine had found its way on to the carpets and several of the clientele. Then Donic's lights went out and his voice ground to a halt. Then his head dropped off into a customer's lap. Just who was the most stupid – Donic, the manufacturer, the owner or the DJ – I'll leave to your judgement. The diners reported that they'd never had such an 'interesting' time before.

Stupidity by the forkful

Pierre Joilot's employers were quite understanding when he backed his forklift truck over the edge of the wharf at Toulouse Docks, where he was employed. It was just one of those things; *c'est la vie* and all that.

However, their understanding wore a little thin when he did it a second time, and a third, and then a fourth, and even a fifth.

It was sixth time unlucky, though, for Joilot: this time they sacked him.

That non-sinking feeling

Peru declared 'Air Force Week' in 1975 and a highlight of the celebrations was a demonstration of the fighter-pilots' skills.

So fourteen old fishing boats were brought out, dusted down, sailed some distance off the coast and abandoned, for the thirty fighter planes to do their stuff.

They flew over the boats, both high and low, bombing, swooping, strafing. The whole thing lasted nearly a quarter of an hour – but not a single boat was sunk.

Guards at Alconte Prison near Lisbon in Portugal must have felt pretty stupid when they allowed what was the largest prison escape ever to occur.

It happened in July 1978. Prison warders noticed that attendances at film shows had fallen (ironically, one of the movies shown was *The Great Escape*!). It was also noticed that 220 knives and large quantities of electric cable were missing. 'We were planning to look for them, but never got around to it,' a guard explained.

What the screws hadn't noticed were the huge holes in a wall, because they were covered with posters. They didn't seem to be aware of the spades, water hoses, electric drills and chisels that began to be seen lying around.

Mind you, one vigilant guard did seem to notice that on the evening before the mass escape there were only 13 prisoners present in his block, when there should have been 36. But, then, some inmates tended to miss roll calls or just hid – for the hell of it.

A warder was quoted as saying, after the breakout, 'We only found out about the escape at 6.30 the next morning when one of the prisoners told us.'

The Justice Minister, Dr Santos Pais, told newspapers that such things were 'normal' and part of the 'legitimate desire of the prisoner to regain his liberty'.

Through a glass quickly

A lawyer was demonstrating the safety of windows in a downtown Toronto skyscraper. Garry Hoy, aged 39, was explaining the strength of the building's windows to visiting law students in 1996

He had previously conducted demonstrations of the windows' strength, said police, by shoulder-charging the glass. This time he went through – and fell 24 floors to his death on the courtyard of the Toronto Dominion Bank Tower.

Unsung hero

A Russian conscript managed to become a 'hero' for the other side when he set three planes on fire. He was driving a de-icing machine in Astrakhan in southern Russia when he crashed into a fighter plane. It caught fire and set alight two others.

The accident destroyed as many Russian planes as had so far been brought down in the country's war in Chechnya. The conscript, who faced a court martial, was hailed a hero by the Chechens – but his own side were definitely not amused.

Who turned out the lights?

A medium-sized warehouse in a west Texas town was evacuated some years ago when employees noticed the smell of a gas leak. All potential sources of ignition – lights, power and so on – were sensibly extinguished or switched off.

After the evacuation two employees of the gas company arrived and upon entering the building found they had to navigate in the semi-dark. None of the lights worked, and they couldn't figure out why.

Later, witnesses looking on from a safe distance outside reported that one of the men pulled something resembling a lighter from his pocket, flicked it and – *boom*! Up went the building. Nothing was found of the technicians, but the lighter was virtually untouched by the blast. It was said that the technician who was suspected of causing the explosion had never been thought of as bright by his peers.

Blast it!

According to the San Jose *Mercury News*, an unidentified man was using a shotgun to wreck the windscreen of a former girlfriend's car. He was wielding it as though it were a club but he accidentally killed himself when the gun discharged, blowing a hole in his gut.

INDETERMINATE INSANITY

Call me stupid, but I couldn't think of one definitive category for this lot. So this is a cop-out. I was going to call this section 'Misc.', but that would have been a *total* cop-out. *And* it sounds boring. Still, there are some good tales – like the chap who tried to insure his cigars against burning or the Frenchman who just couldn't commit suicide – though the Reaper got him anyway.

Kicking up a stink

A businessman in Welwyn Garden City in Hertfordshire was so offended by the smell that came from a sausage-skin factory that he failed to do his homework before going out and buying the entire works.

He intended, of course, to put it to another use – one that would not create such an offensive odour. What he didn't bother to find out first was that it was restricted under a local by-law to certain activities: boiling blood, breeding maggots and making glue and manure.

Backsmith

The clerk at the applications desk at Detroit's License Bureau thought he was being precise when he asked Will Smith to write his name – surname first, first name second.

Smith looked a bit confused at this instruction and said, 'How's that again?'

The clerk – busy and harried – barked, 'Write your name backward.'

So Smith did just as he was told. Mind you, it took him some time to do so because he laboriously wrote, 'lliW htimS'.

Fighting fire with fire

Is this fellow stupid or clever? I'll leave you to make up your own mind – but I reckon anyone claiming fire insurance on his cigars because he smoked them is pretty shrewd. It was a story that featured on that wonderful BBC Radio 4 programme, *The News Quiz*, on 5 May 2000, and was read by the comedian and writer Andy Hamilton in the bit where participants have to read some cuttings. He didn't know which magazine it was from (it had been sent in by a listener), but this is, word for word, what he read:

A man from Charlotte, North Carolina, having purchased a case of very expensive cigars, insured them against, among other things, fire. Within a month, having smoked his entire stockpile, the man filed a claim against the insurance company, stating that the cigars were lost in a series of small fires.

The insurance company refused to pay, citing the obvious reason that the man had consumed the cigars in the normal fashion. The man sued, and won.

In delivering the ruling, the judge, agreeing that the claim was frivolous, stated nevertheless that the man held a policy from the company in which it had warranted that the cigars were insurable and also guaranteed that it would insure against fire, without defining what it considered to be acceptable fire, and was obliged to pay the claim.

Rather than endure a lengthy and costly appeal process, the insurance company accepted the ruling and paid the man $15,000 for the rare cigars he lost in the fires. After he cashed the cheque, however, the company had him arrested on 24 counts of arson.

Cigars all round for that last stroke of genius!

Accidental suicide . . .

Doing a thorough job means having contingencies. Jacques Le Février decided he'd leave nothing to chance when he wanted to top himself.

He stood at the top of a cliff and tied a noose around his neck, having tied the other end of the rope to a rock. Then he drank some poison and set fire to his clothes.

Just in case that little lot didn't work, he decided he would shoot himself at the last moment.

So, poisoned and in flames, he jumped.

He fired the pistol but the bullet missed him and cut through the rope, freeing him from the threat of hanging. He fell straight into the sea and extinguished the flames. Not only that, but swallowing seawater made him throw up – thereby expelling the poison.

He was dragged out of the water by a friendly fisherman and taken to hospital.

Where he died later of exposure.

Light fantastic

A man from Pacoima, Los Angeles, was found dead in 1999 after neighbours reported a bad smell coming from his apartment. Police went into the apartment and saw that every square centimetre of it – including appliances and the inside of the toilet – was covered with pornographic images taken from magazines.

Officer Hradj of the Pacoima Police Department said, 'The visual effect was very unsettling. Because everything looked the same, you could not tell where one wall ended and a doorway began.'

Apparently, the man had also attached a wire frame to his head so he could attach pornographic pictures to it and never have his beloved images out of his sight. But the contraption meant he had no peripheral vision.

The man had picked up a feather duster and had apparently been dusting a hanging lamp – and it was suspended from this that police found him, his wire frame entangled in the lamp. He had choked to death while trying to extricate himself.

Police say the man, who was in his mid-thirties, never left his apartment and had food delivered weekly.

Plenty of bottle

Kenneth Blyton must have imagined himself to be something out of *Enid* Blyton when he decided to cross the English Channel in a metal bottle in the late 1960s. But he did it. The bottle was driven by a small motor and it was his third crossing, although the first one by bottle.

When he landed at Cap Gris Nez, he said, 'I've already crossed by bedstead and by barrel. Next year I intend to cross by giant banana.'

We have no records as to whether the intrepid Mr Blyton managed this.

Oops!

Lord Kelvin should have known better when he made some pronouncements during his time as President of the Royal Society (1890–95).

'Heavier-than-air flying machines are impossible,' he once said. He also said, 'X-rays will prove to be a hoax.' And on another occasion the learned gentleman said, 'Radio has no future.'

Lost souls

Three of the best-known explorers in history – Sir Vivian Fuchs, Robin Hanbury-Tenison and Dr John Hemming – were invited to a dinner at the Geographical Club in London

Fuchs, it may be remembered, explored Greenland and East Africa. He had also led the Commonwealth Trans-Antarctic Expedition of 1955–58.

Hanbury-Tenison had crossed South America in a small boat, and had explored Ecuador, Brazil, Venezuela and much more.

And Hemming was Director of the Royal Geographical Society and had been a member of the Brazilian Expedition of 1961.

However, having met up at the Royal Geographical Society headquarters just a quarter of a mile from the dinner venue, they all got hopelessly lost in Kensington's back streets.

Spliffing tale

Barry Shoemaker of Harlington in Texas got a bit too specific when asked not to smoke in a public place – and it got him arrested.

He went along to a meeting of the Harlington City Commission and watched the proceedings with some interest. Then he decided he'd like a smoke, so lit up.

But there was a no-smoking rule, and the city manager saw him and politely asked him to put out his cigarette. However, Shoemaker went from the frying pan into the fire with the remark, 'It's not a cigarette. It's a joint.'

Princely sum

A fabulously rich Russian nobleman, Prince Urussoff, was a superstitious man and on his honeymoon his new wife lost her wedding ring in the Black Sea.

Prince Urussoff believed that the loss of the wedding ring would mean also the death of the bride. So, in order to keep the ring legally in his possession he spent the equivalent of $40 million buying the shores of the Black Sea.

They say a fool and his money are soon parted. Not so for his family, though: when he died they sold the shores and doubled the money.

The heat got to him

A Californian man decided in 1983 that he wasn't getting a good enough tan. He'd heard that you get a better quality of sun's ray at a certain height –

above the urban smog – so he rigged up helium-filled balloons to his deckchair and anchored himself to the ground with a rope long enough for him to rise to the desired height.

However, his anchor rope snapped, and he rose quickly to about 15,000 feet, where a passing airline pilot reported him as a UFO.

He pulled out an air pistol and shot the balloons one by one until his deckchair descended, demolishing a power cable and plunging the area into blackness.

Oh, the Cologne!

A German man loved to make matchstick models and often entered his creations into competitions. However, in spite of his undoubted skills, he never won a prize.

One year he made a *pièce de résistance* in the form of a beautiful model of Cologne cathedral. It was absolutely perfect – a delight to the eye.

However, he didn't want anything untoward to happen, so he sat up all of the night before the competition to keep an eye on his masterwork. But he fell asleep. He had been smoking a pipe at the time, and it fell into the model, destroying not only his pride and joy but also his house.

He has since given up making models. And smoking!

HAVE I GOT NEWS
FOR YOU

News used to be the ultimate in fact. 'Comment is free, but facts are sacred,' said C. P. Scott (1846–1932), in what was then called the *Manchester Guardian* (though I prefer Tom Stoppard's 'Comment is free but facts are on expenses', but there you go). Now, of course, it's just another commodity – so much so that we have at least two comical quizzes based on it (*Have I Got News For You* on BBC television and *The News Quiz* on Radio 4), not to mention BBC Radio 2's *The News Huddlines* and any number of satire shows based on the news. Where would we be without it?

And here isn't the news . . .

Most newshounds have heard the apocryphal story of the young weekly-newspaper reporter sent to report on a local society wedding. He came back with an empty notebook and told the chief reporter,

'It didn't happen, Chief – nothing to report: some-body shot the bride.'

Well V. S. Pritchett, while better known as a writer and literary critic, tried his hand at reporting hard news for the *Christian Science Monitor*, and once missed the resignation of a cabinet minister, saying he 'couldn't see how it mattered'.

But it was in 1922 that he outdid that. He was sent to Morocco to cover the war there, and said afterwards, 'Any enterprising reporter would have gone into the hills to interview the Moroccan leader Abdul Krin, but not me. The idea filled me with horror and I vigorously abstained. All I heard was a lot of gunfire in the evenings – but it was a lovely country.'

Elementary, my dear Watson!

An idea of two journalists on the *Independent* to investigate the shadowy world of the private detective was perhaps not such a bright one. After all, they would be dealing with, well, *private* detectives.

They used fictitious names and approached a number of private eyes asking them to spy on their editor. However, the sleuths were horrified at the idea, and decided to do an exposé of the exponents of the exposé.

So they watched the two hacks' every move as they stationed themselves in a London hotel. They even spotted that they'd failed to pay for several drinks from the minibar. One of the journos went to use the phone booth at lunchtime, and the private eyes were falling over themselves to get to the booth next door to listen in.

The journalists' own story appeared in the next day's *Independent*. However, they were astounded to read of the detectives' own 'exposé' in the *Observer* the following Sunday.

The e-mail of the species is deadlier than the mail

On BBC Radio 4's *The News Quiz* on 31 March 2000 a cutting was read by Andy Hamilton, the bearded comic who is a regular on the panel. Whether it was a prank because the repeat of the programme would be going out the following day – April Fools' Day – I don't know, but it's worth recounting.

It concerned an American businessman who was travelling south to sunny Florida on a business trip and his wife was due to follow the next day. On arriving in his hotel room, he decided to e-mail his beloved and got to work on his laptop computer. However, he had left his e-mail addresses on his desktop at home, but thought he knew hers anyway, and typed it in. E-mail addresses, though, just aren't like snail-mail addresses, which, if there's a wrong spelling, Postie will correctly interpret. They have to be exact. And our man's was just one letter wrong.

Off went the e-mail at the speed of light and

found its way on to the computer of a rector's wife whose husband had died the previous day. She let out a scream, and her daughter, on rushing into her mother's study, looked aghast at the computer screen. There was an e-mail that read something like this:

Dearest Wife

Have just checked in. Preparations all made for your arrival tomorrow.

Love John.
PS: It sure is hot down here.

Tommy rot

A broadcaster who said he was 'overcome with emotion' was Lieutenant-Commander Tommy Woodroofe, Royal Navy, when he performed a memorable radio commentary on the illumination of the fleet at Spithead. It was 1937, and he'd been having a liquid celebration just before the more public celebrations got under way, and had imbibed a bit too much, by all accounts. Here's what he said – and it was interspersed by pauses lasting up to eleven seconds:

'At the present moment the whole fleet is lit up. When I say lit up I mean lit up by fairy lamps. It's fantastic. It isn't a fleet at all. It's just – it's Fairyland. The whole fleet is in Fairyland. Now, if you'll follow me through . . . if you don't mind . . . the next few moments you'll find the fleet doing odd things. [*Lengthy pause*] I'm sorry – I was telling some people to shut up talking. [*Ships' lights go out so rockets can be fired*] It's gone. It's gone. There's no fleet. It's – it's disappeared. No magician who ever could have waved his wand could have waved it with more acumen than he has now at the present moment. The fleet's gone. It's disappeared. I was talking to you in the middle of this – damn [*he coughs*] – in the middle of this fleet and what's happened is the fleet's gone and disappeared and gone.'

Suddenly, Commander Woodroofe's voice was curtailed, and a polite announcer said 'That is the end of the Spithead commentary.' Then there was dance music.

ROYALS, RULERS AND OTHER UNDESIRABLES

Let's face it, they're fair game. They set themselves up to be victims of the slings and arrows of outrageous humour, and we take advantage of it. Probably because we find it hard to trust anyone who has power over us.

Like the US President who was forbidden to make his speech because it was too boring, or Idi Amin. Needn't really say anything more about him, need we?

Pipped at the poll

When Herbert Connolly fought to keep his seat on the Massachusetts Governor's Council he campaigned vigorously – so much so that when he got to the polling booth to cast his own vote for himself it was closed. Polling had stopped fifteen minutes earlier.

However, he got a good poll: 14,715. Unfortunately, his opponent got 14,716.

Right royal perfectionist

The Russian Tsar Paul (1754–1801) was consumed with the idea that his soldiers should look just so – even if that meant their efficiency was severely compromised.

They had to wear tight-fitting uniforms – which meant they could hardly breathe – and he insisted they wear straitjackets under their uniforms to ensure they remained erect.

They also had to wear thick heavy wigs that had iron rods in them to make them sit straight on the head, and they had to have steel plates strapped to their knees to prevent their legs from bending when they marched.

Presidential prattle

William Henry Harrison (1773–1841) was the ninth President of the USA – but never got around to doing anything. He had written a speech to use at his inauguration in 1841 that was so long and boring that his own party, the Whigs, banned him from delivering it!

It was culled largely from schoolboy memories of Plutarch, and General Harrison was quite proud of it. However, Daniel Webster, the lexicographer, was brought in to rewrite it – and even then it lasted an hour and 40 minutes and needed 91-column inches (232 centimetres) of the *New York Evening Post* to contain it.

But Harrison had delivered the address on the coldest day of the year without a hat or coat, and he caught pneumonia and died just one month after his inauguration.

Idi-ocy

Few people would deny that Idi Amin was one of the stupidest rulers of modern times. The man who once refused to attend the Commonwealth Games unless the British Queen sent him a new pair of size-13 boots, turned out to be insane. He once volunteered to marry Princess Anne.

He also invited the former British Prime Minister, Edward Heath, to take his band to Uganda to help him celebrate the anniversary of his military coup, and remarked on Heath's demotion to the obscure rank of bandleader. (Edward Heath is, of course, a musician and conductor, but there is also a bandleader called Ted Heath.) He then offered to supply Britain with some goats and chickens.

On another occasion, he offered the British a shipload of vegetables to ease the recession.

The crackpot dictator gave dinner guests a surprise at his state house in Entebbe in August 1972. Suddenly he got up, went to the kitchen and emerged carrying the frozen head of his former commander-in-chief, Brigadier Hussein.

Amin proceeded to scream abuse at the head, and threw cutlery at it. Then he asked all the guests to leave.

Two of this extraordinary man's hobbies were erecting statues all over the country to his greatest idols, Queen Victoria and Adolf Hitler, and crushing men's genitals with his bare hands.

Then, in 1978, Amin decided he'd like to mount a full-scale invasion of Tanzania. However, he needed to lull its president, Julius Nyerere, into a false sense of security, so he sent him a telegram: 'I love you so much that if you were a woman I would consider marrying you.'

Right royal stupidity

There's an English legend about a bunch of fools who weren't so daft – the villagers of Gotham in Nottinghamshire.

They were threatened by a visit from King John (1199–1216) and weren't too keen on the idea because of the expense it would entail, so they pretended to be stupid. When royal messengers arrived they found the Wise Men of Gotham engaged in the most outrageous behaviour, such as joining hands around a thorn three to trap a cuckoo and trying to drown an eel.

Unsurprisingly, His Majesty decided to stay elsewhere. The 'foles of Gotham' are mentioned in the fifteenth-century Wakefield plays, and a collection of their antics was published in the sixteenth century as *Merrie Tales of the Mad-Men of Gottam*.

SEX

More jokes are told about sex than any other subject. We can be prurient in so many different ways, from harmless humour to being dead kinky.

Did you hear the one about the guy with the hot apple pie? Laugh? *He* didn't!

Hard luck!

A Guyana newspaper carried the story in 1999 of a chap who wanted to prolong an erection for a date with his girlfriend, so he took – or, rather, overdosed on – a drug called cantarden, usually used for putting horses on heat.

It worked OK and the man had – to his horror – the most painful erection, and couldn't get rid of it.

When, after some days, he went for medical help he thought he could keep the whole thing quiet, but it was not to be. Word got out and he was the laughing stock of his town, where he got the nickname 'staff sergeant'.

Eventually, after three weeks of this humiliation, he underwent surgery, but discovered then that he could no longer get it up!

Just dessert?

Apparently fancying a bit of hot sex, an Idaho teenager decided in March 2000 to imitate a scene from the hit movie *American Pie* and got a nasty shock.

He was trying to have sexual intercourse with a hot apple pie – and we all know how hot cooked apple is when it's . . . well, when it's hot! It's *bloody* hot – that's how hot it is.

Poor Dwight Emburger, aged 17, was rushed to hospital with serious burns to his penis, which was left somewhat scarred.

He just couldn't wait till the pie had cooled before satisfying his odd sexual fantasy.

Sex drive

Reuters reported in 1999 on a Romanian First Division soccer player, Mario Bugeanu, who died with his girlfriend Mirela Iancu after they'd had sex in his car. Unfortunately, 24-year-old Bugeanu and 23-year-old Iancu had not thought to turn off the engine. Since the car was in the garage, carbon monoxide built up and the amorous pair were poisoned.

They were discovered by the player's father the following day.

Shocking business

A woman police officer from Ohio responded to a call from someone who said his father was not breathing. She found the man face down on the couch, naked. When she rolled him over to check his pulse and to begin cardiopulmonary resuscitation, she noticed burn marks on his genitals.

The man was DOA at hospital, but meanwhile police gave the couch a thorough investigation. They noticed that the man had made a hole between the cushions, so they flipped the couch over and saw what had caused his death.

It turned out that he had a habit of putting his penis between the cushions, down into the hole and between two electric sanders – with the sandpaper removed, of course. The story goes that, after his orgasm, his discharge shorted out one of the sanders, and he was electrocuted.

THIS SPORTING LIFE

While women like sport and get on with it quietly for the enjoyment of it, men like to shout about it and make total prats of themselves into the bargain. You only have to see some old footage of John McEnroe to see that. You can trust men to bring something to sport that most of us wish it had never had – like total idiocy.

Take the loudmouth who took on Billie Jean King and was made to look a total berk. Or the practice of 'pumping', which we won't go into in this civilized little introduction. But be warned . . .

I've included one or two other leisure activities and pastimes in this section, but to have a heading that said 'This sporting, leisure and other pastimes life' would have been *totally* stupid.

King's pawn

Male chauvinists are usually pretty stupid, too. Bobby Riggs certainly was when he challenged Billie Jean King to a battle-of-the-sexes tennis match.

Riggs hadn't been a Wimbledon champion since 1939, and this was 1973, but he was determined to beat this member of the sex which, he said, were at their prettiest when barefoot, pregnant, taking care of the children and working in the home.

'I want to set women's lib back twenty years, to get women back in the home where they belong,' he declared. 'I will scrape her up. She is a woman and is subject to women's emotional frailties. She will crack up during the match.'

And so the largest crowd thus far in tennis history – about 39,000 people – gathered to watch the match. King thrashed him 6–4, 6–3, 6–3.

Boxing not so clever

Harvey Gartley managed to become the first boxer to save his opponent the job of knocking him out. He did it himself.

Gartley was fighting in the regional bantamweight heats of the 15th annual Saginaw Golden Gloves contest in Michigan, and his opponent was Dennis Oulette. Both boxers were quite nervous, as neither had fought in public before.

Gartley came out of his corner, doing the usual bobbing and weaving, and the crowd roared. However, as Gartley closed in he threw a punch and promptly fell down. He was exhausted. And he stayed down for a count of ten!

End of the line

A Canadian angler was fishing in one of the country's many lakes and was ecstatic to find he'd landed a humongous pike. He quickly dispatched it with a stick and laid it on the bank beside his shotgun.

However, the fish was not as dead as our angler friend thought and began to thrash about. Its tail caught on the trigger and . . .

You've guessed it. Whether the fish managed to thrash itself back into the water we'll never know, but the angler didn't live to tell the tale.

Bull week

In Betulia, Colombia, they took 'amateur night' a bit too far. The town's annual carnival includes five days of amateur bullfighting. No bull was killed in 1999 – but dozens of would-be matadors were hurt, including one who was gored in the head and one who had his willy half gouged off.

One participant said, 'It's just one bull against a town of a thousand morons.' Those who feel that bullfighting is an abomination would be inclined to agree.

Depths of stupidity

A subaqua club in the West Country of England wanted to dive in Britain's least accessible loch in a remote part of Scotland, and duly sought permission. Permission granted, off they went, knowing they would be the first people to explore this far-off lake.

They drove 740 miles and climbed 3,000 feet. Then they donned their diving gear and in they went – to find the lake was only four foot deep.

One step beyond

Changes in the vernacular can lead us to all sorts of conclusions. See what you make of this.

This guy was obviously into jogging in a big way, yet his wife said the 49-year-old San Francisco stockbroker was 'totally zoned' when, during his daily run, he accidentally jogged a bit too far – and went right over the edge of a 200-foot cliff.

Zoned?

Stretching a point . . .

A 22-year-old man from Fairfax County in the US state of Virginia was using those stretchy luggage ropes with hooks on the ends – you know, the sort you use on your car's roof rack – to bungee-jump. Eric A. Barcia, a fast-food worker, leaped off a 70-foot (21-metre) railway bridge with the tied-together ropes attached to his foot.

And hit the pavement.

A police spokesman, Warren Carmichael, said,

'The length of the cord that he had assembled was greater than the distance between the trestle [of the bridge] and the ground.'

Fire down below

In the mid-1990s, a firework proved the undoing of 28-year-old Daniel Wyman of Illinois, who drowned in Fox Lake after he and his companion blew a hole in the bottom of their aluminium rowing boat.

The firework is known as an M-250. It packs about a quarter of the punch of a stick of dynamite.

Danny and his buddy threw the M-250 into the water near their 14-foot boat but a sudden gust of wind blew the boat right over it.

Danny's friend swam to shore and was taken to Northern Illinois Medical Center in McHenry for observation. But Danny couldn't swim. Nor had the pair taken any lifesaving equipment with them.

Getting carried away

The trainer of the American soccer team got distracted by his own emotions when, during the 1930 semi-final against Argentina, he dashed on to the field to tend an injured player.

Argentina had just scored a goal that was disputed, and our man decided to shout abuse at the referee as he was dashing past.

However, in his fit of temper he got to the injured

man, threw down his medical bag and broke a bottle of chloroform. By this single act, he managed to anaesthetize himself and had to be carried off by his own team.

Hammer horror

In 1952 the hammer thrower at an athletics event in the north-east of England broke some records – and a few other things as well.

He swirled the hammer around and let go, and off it went, landing outside the enclosure – right on the bonnet of his Triumph Spitfire, which he had arranged to sell that night. That cost him £150 to put right

But things didn't stop there, for it bounced off the car and through the window of the stadium office, knocking an official unconscious.

The thrower wasn't new to this special skill, however: he had on previous occasions hit a petrol station, a gents' toilet – from which a spectator emerged hurriedly, thinking it had been struck by lightning – and a police car

Hook, line and that sinking feeling

Organizers of the National Ambulance Service fishing championships at Kidderminster, in what is now Herefordshire, in 1972 forgot to tell the 200 expected participants of one vital fact. On the appointed day, the anglers turned up and cast their lines. All day they sat, and not one of them got a bite.

Eventually a local passed by and informed them that they were wasting their time: the fish had all been moved to other waters three weeks before.

Inflation figure

Below is a rather disgusting story of one young man's stupidity. It may disturb some readers, so if you're of a nervous disposition please look away while you're reading it. It's from the *Japan Times* of 16 April 1997:

> ' "Pumping",' a spokesman for the Nakhon Ratchasima hospital told reporters. 'If this perversion catches on, it will destroy the cream of Thailand's manhood.'
>
> He was speaking after the remains of 13-year-old Charnchai Puanmuangpak bad been rushed into the hospital's emergency room. 'Most "Pumpers" use a standard bicycle pump,' he explained, 'inserting the nozzle far up their rectum, giving themselves a rush of air, creating a momentary high. This act is a sin against God.'
>
> It appears that the young Charnchai took it further still. He started using a two-cylinder foot pump, but even that wasn't exciting enough for him, so he boasted to friends that he was going to try the compressed air hose at a nearby gasoline station. They dared him to do it, so, under cover of darkness, he

snuck in. Not realizing how powerful the machine was, he inserted the tube deep into his rectum, and placed a coin in the slot. As a result, he died virtually instantly, leaving passers-by still in shock.

One woman thought she was watching a twilight fireworks display, and started clapping. 'We still haven't located all of him,' say the police authorities. 'When that quantity of air interacted with the gas in his system, he nearly exploded. It was like an atom bomb went off or something.'

'Pumping is the devil's pastime, and we must all say no to Satan,' Ratchasima concluded. 'Inflate your tires by all means, but then hide your bicycle pump where it cannot tempt you.'

It would certainly put the wind up me!

Tree cheers for Tom!

The eighteenth-century scholar Thomas Birch decided that, because he was such a keen fisherman but never caught any fish, he would do something radical to assure the fish that he was of no harm to them. He decided to disguise himself as a tree.

So he made an outfit that allowed his arms to fit into the branches and his eyes to peep through two holes in the bark. And off he went to the river and positioned himself in the likeliest spot from which he no doubt hoped he would make the biggest catch of his angling career so far.

However, all he managed to catch was the occasional dog needing a pee and a few people who thought here was a good place to have a picnic.

Whether he styled his disguise to reflect his surname we do not know.

Late kick-off

In 1974 Mombasa Rugby Football Club boarded a plane and flew the 475 miles to Uganda for their annual needle match with Nairobi Harlequins. Little did they know that several thousand feet below them, travelling in the opposite direction, were a fleet of cars bound for Mombasa.

Each team, once arrived, rang the other to find out where it had got to.

Knockout display

Richard Procter, a featherweight boxer, gave his audience more than enough for their money when he stepped smartly into the ring at the World Sporting Club in London.

With aplomb he slipped off his gown and threw it into the corner. It took a while for him to realize that the sudden burst of cheers, applause and whistling could not be for his fighting prowess – which wasn't yet on show. Only when he looked down did he realize he'd left his shorts in the dressing room.

Mr Sandman

Daniel Jones dug an 8-foot-deep (2.5-metre) hole in the beach at Buxton, North Carolina, in 1998. Twenty-one-year-old Jones had, said beachgoers, dug the hole for fun, or maybe protection from the wind. He had been sitting in a beach chair at the bottom of his hole when the sand caved in, burying him under five feet of the stuff.

People used their hands and shovels to try to get to Jones, of Woodbridge, Virginia, but couldn't reach him in time to save him.

Own goal

Phil Boyce was looking forward to refereeing the local soccer match in Shrewsbury. Unfortunately, he managed to lock himself in the changing rooms, and was stranded there, wondering what to do.

Fortunately for Phil, a linesman's flag came to the rescue. He waved it furiously out of the window until someone saw it, and he was freed from his predicament. The match got going twenty minutes late.

Staggering stupidity

Not so much a sportsman as a poacher – although he was indulging illegally in the sport of stag shooting – Marino Malerba forgot the effects of gravity, which tends to be just the same in Spain as anywhere else.

For this is where Marino met his nemesis. The stag he shot was above him, standing on a rock ledge. As it fell, antlers first, the inevitable happened. The poacher was well and truly skewered and died instantly.

Stupidity's slippery slope

A man died at Mammoth Lakes in California in 1999 when he hit a lift tower in the ski area while riding down the slope on a foam pad. Twenty-two-year-old Matthew David Hubal was dead on arrival an Ventinela Mammoth Hospital.

That afternoon Hubal and his friends had hiked up a ski run called Stump Alley. There they undid the yellow foam protectors from the lift towers, according to Lieutenant Mike Donnelly of the Mammoth Lakes Police Department. The pads, he explained, are used to protect skiers who might hit the towers. The group of men had used the pads, it seemed, to slide down the ski slope and Hubal had crashed into a tower. It was discovered that the tower he hit was one with its pad removed.

The one that did get away!

Franc Filipic was passionate about fishing. So much so that, on one particular fishing expedition in

1996, he caught a big one and was determined that it would not be the one that got away. Unfortunately for the 47-year-old from Ljubljana, Slovenia, he'd caught a powerful specimen known as a sheatfish, much like a catfish.

According to the state-run news agency, the fish pulled Franc under as – according to a friend who was with him – he uttered his last words: 'Now I've got him!' His body was found after a two-day search.

The fish? It got away.

Trails and tribulations

The stupid person of this tale isn't known, but it's worth the telling. He (or perhaps it was a she) was a cartographer with the extraordinary capacity for being truly asinine – unless his intention was to put to the test the proficiency of his map's users, who were footpath walkers.

Ramblers found when using the 1969 'definitive' map in the Dales National Park that one footpath went straight up a cliff face, while another went right through a hospital ward. A third would take walkers through the River Ribble in two places without a bridge.

The *Guardian* said of the map that anyone 'determined to follow the line would have had to wade across the river up to his neck, walk for 200 metres along the eastern bank, and then wade back again'.

Oh, heck!

Just what the little millipede did to deserve the honour of meeting his death at the hands of a crack shot like Jason Heck, we'll never know, but, heck! this is a heck of a guy.

Jason fancied himself as a sharpshooter, and in October 1998 he tried to kill the millipede with a shot from a .22 rifle

However, the little bullet ricocheted off a rock near the hole where the millipede was minding its own business, and hit Jason's pal Antonio Martinez in the head, fracturing his skull.

At this stage we don't know which of the millipede's legs our heck of a sharpshooter was aiming for.

Worst in their field

A television documentary in the late 1970s recorded the achievements of a rugby team from Doncaster in South Yorkshire. During its life, the side came bottom of its league more times than any other club, and lost forty games on the trot.

Once, a topless streaker ran across the field during an away game, so Doncaster advertised in their local paper for a woman with a 42-inch bust to do the same for home matches.

Once the players failed to recognize their own strip because they were covered in mud, and began to tackle their own side.

The entire team was put up for sale in 1980.

It was comparable with the New York Mets, a baseball team formed in 1962. They got a traditional American tickertape welcome down Broadway, with 40,000 spectators and a band – and this was all before they'd ever played.

So they felt pretty stupid when they did play, and proved to be a total disaster. Within a week they had lost nine games in a row – something achieved up till them only by the Brooklyn Dodgers in 1918. They went on to lose more matches in one season than anyone else in the history of the game – the final figure being 120 defeats.

He got the point

In 1999 doctors in Portland, Oregon, said a 25-year-old man who lost his right eye was lucky to be alive, after an initiation into a men's rafting club went horribly wrong.

The club is called Mountain Men Anonymous, based in Grant's Pass, Oregon. The ceremony involved the shooting of a beer can from Tony Roberts's head with a hunting arrow. But the arrow entered Roberts's right eye, and, had it gone just a millimetre to the left, a major blood vessel would have been cut and he would have died instantly.

Dr Johnny Delashaw of the University Hospital in Portland said the arrow had gone through eight to ten inches (20–25 centimetres) of brain.

Roberts said afterwards, 'I feel so dumb about this'.